Contents

Answer keys are online at:
http://cambridge.org/funresources

Home FUN booklet

Jane Ritter

Animals

snail

skateboard

1 **Draw lines from the words to the pictures.**

panda   kangaroo   penguin   bear   dolphin
rabbit   bat   shark   fly   whale   lion   parrot

2 **Write the animals in the best place.**

I fly	I swim	I jump	I am big
bat			

3 **Read and write the name of the animal.**

This animal is very small. It lives in a very small home.
It eats cheese. It has a tail and a pink nose.
What is it? ....

This animal has no legs and no arms. It is long. It eats mice
and eggs. It makes the noise 'sssssssss'.
What is it? ....

This animal has a soft body and a hard shell. It is slow.
Birds eat it.
What is it? ....

4 **Which animal is different? Why?**

Draw four animals. One is different. Tell your family why.

5 Draw your favourite animal.
Talk to your family about your animal.

My favourite animal is … .
It is … . (big / small)
It eats … . (meat / vegetables)
It can … . (fly / swim / jump)

 abc ✓

How do you spell the word?

 d _ _ _ _ _ _ _

The Body and face

1 Find the words and write them.

1 ....hair........
2 ....
3 ....
4 ....
5 ....

o	p	f	s	a	e	b	g	x	n
d	m	o	u	s	t	a	c	h	e
f	e	o	s	h	g	c	j	a	c
o	r	t	z	o	u	k	n	i	k
t	e	e	t	u	r	e	s	r	p
e	a	d	o	l	v	o	d	w	r
a	r	m	x	d	l	s	m	e	i
k	a	g	f	e	e	t	u	y	t
e	m	z	o	r	g	q	k	e	n

6 ....
7 ....
8 ....
9 ....
10 ....

2 Read and find the correct monster.

Complete the text about the monster.

My name is Eddy. I am blue. I've got .....four red..... feet,
.... red eyes and black .... I haven't got any
.... I have got .... blue ears. I'm smiling.

3 Read and draw the monster's face.

My name's Gino. I've got a round blue face and short, curly yellow hair.
I haven't got any ears so I can't hear you. I can see you with my four big green eyes. I've got two small noses under my eyes. I've got a big purple mouth and six small grey teeth.

4 **Fun at home** Find a photo of your friend.

Tell your family about the photo.

This is … .
She's / He's got … eyes. (brown / green / blue)
She's / He's got … hair. (long / short) (straight / curly)
He's / She's … . (tall / short) (fat / thin)

abc ✓

How do you spell the words?

picture	letters	correct spelling
	h e l l o	hello
	b e u u i l f t a	
	e l i k	
	w i t e h	
	b l u e	

5

Numbers

1 Match the words and numbers.

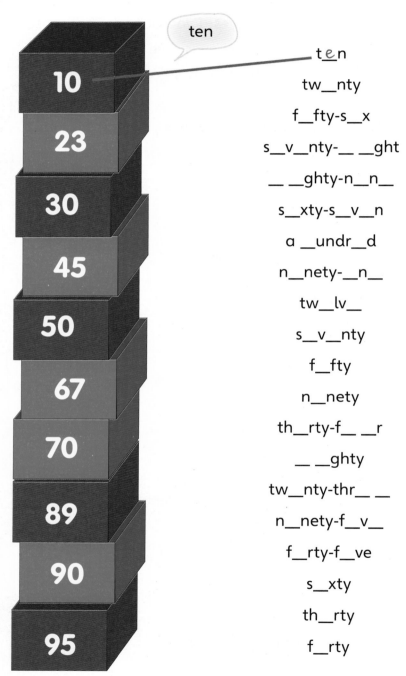

ten

t_e_n

tw__nty

f__fty-s__x

s__v__nty-__ __ght

__ __ghty-n__n__

s__xty-s__v__n

a __undr__d

n__nety-__n__

tw__lv__

s__v__nty

f__fty

n__nety

th__rty-f__ __r

__ __ghty

tw__nty-thr__ __

n__nety-f__v__

f__rty-f__ve

s__xty

th__rty

f__rty

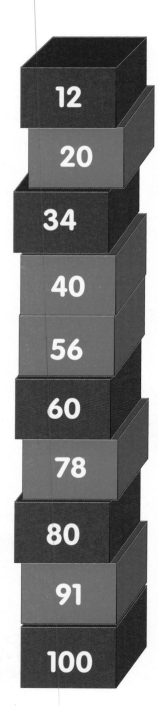

2 Write the letters.

3 Say the numbers.

4 Write the letters and the numbers. What are the answers?

a ⬜26⬜ tw_e_nty-s_i_x + ⬜64⬜ s_i_xty-f_o_ _u_r = ⬜ _ . _ _ _ _ _ _

b ⬜ f_rty-f_v_ + ⬜ th_rt_ _n = ⬜ _ _ _ _ _ _ - _ _ _ _ _

c ⬜ _ _ghty -_n_ + ⬜ n_n_t_ _n = ⬜ a _ _ _ _ _ _ _

5 Read.

> My name is Daisy. Here are my favourite numbers. I live at ninety-eight Smith Street. There are four people in my family. I am ten and my mum is thirty-five years old. My birthday is on the nineteenth of January. I don't like number thirteen. It isn't a good number.

Write the numbers Daisy says:

98					~~13~~

6 Write five of your favourite numbers and one number you don't like. Tell your family why.

....	....	....	....	....	....

> I like the number ... because ... .

> I don't like the number ... because ... .

abc ✓

How do you spell the word?

100 a h _ _ _ _ _ _ _

Family

1 **Read and write the family words.**

I'm Tony. This is my family. My grandmother's name is Ella and my grandfather's name is Tom. They have two children – Nick and Kim. Nick is my dad. My mum's name is Sue. I have got a sister and a brother. Their names are Anna and George. Kim is my aunt. Her husband's name is Peter. They have one son, Paul. He's my cousin.

1 Tom is my *grandfather* .

2 Sue is my ....

3 Kim is Tom and Ella's ....

4 George is my ....

5 Nick is my ....

6 → Anna is my ....

6 ↓ Nick is Tom and Ella's

....

7 Ella is my ....

8 Kim is my ....

9 Peter is my ....

Crossword:
1 g r a n d f a t h e r (down)
3 a ...
5 a t
6 ...
7 r
8 ...
9 ...

2 **Read and complete the text with the words.**

> aunt   cousin   ~~sister~~   grandad   uncle

Jack is at the hospital with his family. They are waiting for Jack's dad. Jack is with his mum, Mary, and his ....*sister*........ Lily. Lily is reading a comic and listening to music. Mary's father, Fred is with them. He is talking on his phone. He is Jack's .... Jane is Mary's sister. She is Jack's .... She is holding a baby. Her husband, Peter, and their baby Sally are waiting too. Peter is Jack's .... and Sally is Jack's ....

3 **Look at Jack's family. Draw lines.**

Mary   Fred   Sally   Jack

Lily   Jane   Peter

4 **Draw your family.**

Write three sentences about your family.

1 I've got ....

2 My ....'s name is

....

3 We live ....

abc ✓

Draw a picture. Remember the spellings.

	brother		person
	child		grandmother
	family		friends

Cover the words, look at the pictures and spell the words.

Food and drink

1 Find the words. Write the words on the lines.

p o$_s$u^u	c j i e^u	k s m l h^{imah} e i a k	c r i e c m e a
soup	....	....	....

t e r w a l o m e n	m i l e	g e r b r u	a m o g n
....	....	....	....

r r c o t s a	s n a e b	g e r p a s	s a e p
....	....	....	....

s g e g	c e s n a p k a
....	....

2 Put the words in groups.

hot	cold	fruit	vegetables
soup			

3 **Read and answer the questions.**

These are made from flour. You eat them hot with meat and vegetables for lunch or dinner. What are they? ....

These have a lot of sugar in them. You eat them at special times. They are very sweet. What are they? ....

This is a drink. It is hot and brown. People add sugar and milk to it. What is it? ....

Food I like

4 What's in the picture?
What's your favourite fruit?

5 Fun at home What's in the kitchen.

- Go to your kitchen.
- Find ten foods or drinks that you like.
- Write the words on stickers:

bananas

lemonade

- Put the stickers on the things you see.
- Test your family.

What's this?

What are those?

Health

1 What are the missing letters? Write words.

t_o_ _o_th_a_ch_e_

_ _ _r_ch_

h_ _ _d_ch_

c_l_

st_m_ch - _ch_

b_ck_ch_

t_mp_r_t_r_

s_r_ _rm

2 Read and answer the questions.

a I can't point to things or write. It's difficult to wave. What's the matter? ......_I've got a sore arm._.......

b I need some water. It's difficult to talk and eat. What's the matter? ....

c I can't walk very well. One shoe is too small for my foot. What's the matter? ....

3 What's in the picture? Tell your family.

Paul is sick.

He is ....

He has got a ....

There is ....

My health

4 Draw your body.

Think about when you were sick, ill or hurt yourself.

Colour aches yellow.

Colour sore things red.

Colour broken things green.

Tell your family about your body.

In my picture I have got a sore... and a broken...

The home

1 **Draw lines from words to pictures.**

desk   armchair   bed   rug   cupboard

computer   window   bookcase

2 **Find four differences and write sentences.**

Picture A	Picture B
The desk is blue.	The desk is green.

3 **Read and draw.**

Draw a yellow toothbrush.

Draw a green towel.

Draw orange toothpaste.

Draw a blue shower.

Draw a purple mat.

Circle the correct answer.

1. The bathroom is upstairs / downstairs.

2. We eat / wash in the bathroom.

14

4 Find a picture of a room in a magazine or on the internet. Glue the picture here. Label the picture.

....

....

....

....

....

....

5 Draw the bedroom you would like to have. Write about it.

This is the bedroom I'd like to have.

It has got ....

It is .... (big / small)

It is .... (colour)

It has got ....

It hasn't got ....

abc ✓

How do you spell the words?

c _ _ _ _ _ _ _

m _ _ _ _ _

Places and directions

1 Look at the pictures and write the words.

park   market   swimming pool   bank   ~~cinema~~
supermarket   farm   library

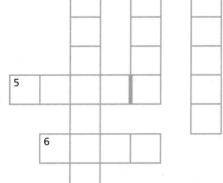

2 Write the places in the best group.

inside	outside
	farm

3 **Look at the map and complete it with the words.**

a) I am next to the shopping centre and opposite the hospital. Where am I?
...... *cinema* ......

b) I am next to the café and opposite the library. Where am I? ....

c) I am next to the station and opposite the supermarket. Where am I?
....

d) I am next to the bank and opposite the swimming pool. Where am I?
....

e) I am between the cinema and the supermarket and opposite the café.
Where am I? ....

My dream town

4 **Fun at home** Draw a map of your dream town.

[blank box]

Write three sentences.

1 There's ....
2 There are ....
3 There is a ....
   opposite the ....

Talk to your family about your dream town.

What is there in your perfect town?

There's a games store.

Sports and leisure

1 Look at the pictures and write the words.

c <u>o</u> <u>o</u> k

s _ _ l

w _ _ k

c _ _ l

c _ _ _ b

t _ _ _ _ s

p _ _ _ t

d _ _ _ e

l _ u _ h

b _ _ k _ _ b _ _ l

Which word is not a sport or leisure word? ....

2 Read, match and answer.

You do this sport in a pool. You move your arms and legs in the water.
What is it? ....

You go to a shopping centre and buy things. Sometimes you have a lot of bags.
What is it? ....

You use a mobile phone to do this. You send messages to your friends.
What is it? ....

You do this sport in a boat. The wind moves your boat.
What is it? ....

18

3 Which picture is different? Why?

① ② ③

① ② ③

① ② ③

Draw three activities (one is different).

Tell your family why ...

This picture is different because ... .

The sport / place is ... .

The children are ... .

4 Fun at home Find pictures of three sports you like and glue them in your book. Write why you like them.

	I like .... because ....
	I like ....
	....

Time

1 Can you remember the days of the week? Write the words.

Monday
Tuesday
Wednesday
Thursday
Friday
Saturday
Sunday

1 This day is after Monday. ....Tuesday......

2 This day is before Sunday. ....

3 This day is between Tuesday and Thursday.

....

4 This day is before Saturday. ....

5 This day is between Sunday and Tuesday.

....

6 This day is after Wednesday. ....

7 This day is before Monday. ....

2 What did Tom do on his holiday? Find and write.

Tuesday   Thursday   Saturday

1 On Tuesday he ......went sailing........ .

2 On Thursday he ....

3 On Saturday he ....

20

3 **Read and write the days under the pictures.**

Vicky's Holiday

Vicky went to a farm for her holiday. She had a fantastic time. She went there with her family on Saturday. On Sunday, she rode her bike to the town. It was beautiful. On Tuesday, they went to a lake near the village and she went out in a boat. Her favourite day was Friday, when she rode a horse. It was a fantastic holiday.

..... Friday ....

4 **Find and glue in three pictures from your holiday. Write about your holiday.**

On my holiday I ....

....

....

....

5 **What did they do on holiday? Find the words and write.**

.... played football ....

....

School

1 Find the words and match them to the pictures.

internet   board   playground   ~~teacher~~   tick
desk   write   spell   draw   question

a-p-p-l-e

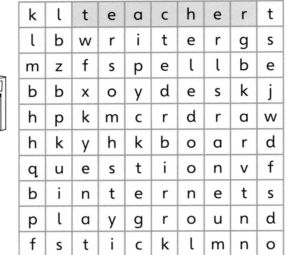

k	l	t	e	a	c	h	e	r	t
l	b	w	r	i	t	e	r	g	s
m	z	f	s	p	e	l	l	b	e
b	b	x	o	y	d	e	s	k	j
h	p	k	m	c	r	d	r	a	w
h	k	y	h	k	b	o	a	r	d
q	u	e	s	t	i	o	n	v	f
b	i	n	t	e	r	n	e	t	s
p	l	a	y	g	r	o	u	n	d
f	s	t	i	c	k	l	m	n	o

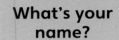
What's your name?

2 What is it? Read and write.

Sometimes we read a story or write some sentences.
We do this at home, not at school.
What is it? It's h.<u>omework</u> .

This is a book with pictures and words. It's about real
or not real people and things and it is fun to read.
What is it? It's a s...................... .

Sometimes the answer is not correct. We don't tick
the answer.
What is it? It's a m...................... .

frog

My school

3 Write words you know and draw lines.

board

Tell your family about your classroom:

How many desks are there?

Is there a ...?

Is it big or small?

Are there any ...?

What colour is the ...?

Ten.

Yes. / No.

It's ... . (colour)

abc

How do you spell the words?

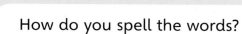 m _ _ _ _

 h _ _ _ _ _ _ _ _

Transport

1 Look at the pictures and write the words.

2 What's wrong? Correct the mistakes.

He's flying a motorbike.

.......He's.. riding.. a........

.............motorbike.............

She's riding a plane.

....

....

He's flying a bike.

....

....

She's riding a lorry.

....

....

He's driving a helicopter.

....

....

3 Find six differences. Write sentences.

Picture A	Picture B
There isn't a lorry.	There is a lorry.

4 Read and complete the text with the words.

Clare's dream car

fly   watch   drive   ~~go~~   trip   go

This is my dream car. It has special wheels that ....go.......... everywhere. When you are late, it transforms into a helicopter and it can .... When you .... on a long .... there is a tablet and cinema. Six people can travel in the car. I love this car, it's brilliant!

5 Draw your dream car or other transport. Tell your family.

It can / can't ... .

It is ... (colour).

It is ... (size).

25

Weather

1 Look at the pictures and write the words.

s <u>n</u> <u>o</u> <u>w</u>   r _ _ _   r _ _ _ _ _ _   h _ _   w _ _ _ _

  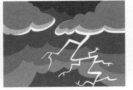  

s _ _ _ _   w _ _   s _ _ _ _ _   d _ _   i _ _

2 Read and circle the correct word.

It is sun / (sunny) / sunniest today.

1

I like playing in the snow / snowy / snowiest.

2

The rain / rainy / rainiest place on Earth is in India.

3

The dry / driest / drier place on Earth is in Chile.

4

It is very cloud / cloudy / cloudiest today.

5

The wind / windy / windiest place on earth is Antarctica.

3 Read, draw, colour and complete the text.

Draw a boat. Colour it ....*orange*.......... and ....
The fish are ....
Draw a boy in the boat.
He's wearing a .... coat and a .... hat.
The sun is ....
The clouds are ....
Draw a rainbow.

My weather

4 Fun at home What can you see from your window? Tell your family.

What's the weather like?

...*It's* hot / cold.

... sunny / windy / snowy.

I can see ... .

I'm wearing ... .

abc ✓

How do you spell the words?

   d _ _ _ _ _ _

   w _ _ _ _ _ _

The world around us

1 Match the words, pictures and meanings.

town   This is bigger than a village. People live there.

leaves   This is a forest in a hot country. There are lots of trees, plants and animals.

star   This has water in it. It starts in the mountains and finishes at the sea.

river   This is white and round. You see it at night.

moon   This is smaller than a town. People live there.

village   This is small and white. There are many in the sky at night.

jungle   There is water all round this. Britain is one.

island   These grow on trees. In the autumn they go red and yellow and fall.

2 Look at the picture. Write the words.

f _i_ _e_ _l_ _d_   r _ _ _   s _ _

l _ _ _   g _ _ _ _ _

What's in the picture? Tell your family.

3 **Read and write the words.**

cafés river roads parks ~~city~~ world

London is a very big (1).........city......... .
There is a famous (2)..................... called
the Thames. You can see it in this picture.
There are hundreds of (3).....................
which cars, buses, lorries and motorbikes
go on. I think it's the best city in the
(4)..................... . There are beautiful green
(5)..................... where you can relax and
have lunch or sit and read. You can also
find hundreds of (6)..................... where
you can sit and watch the world go by.

sky

the London Eye

river

Big Ben

The world around me

4 **Fun at home** Find a picture of your town. Glue the picture here.
Label your picture. Tell your family.

This is my town / village / city.

There's a … .

There are … .

It's big / small.

It's old / new.

abc ✓

How do you spell the words ?

 m _ _ _ _ _ _

 w _ _ _ _ _ _ _

Adjectives

1 Find the words and match them to the pictures.

h	y	c	s	u	d	j	z	i	h	o	t
d	z	u	k	m	c	l	e	a	n	b	z
k	r	e	f	b	i	l	r	m	e	n	k
n	u	b	e	a	u	t	i	f	u	l	y
t	s	h	o	r	t	w	s	t	u	k	h
x	f	t	f	o	y	c	o	l	d	n	l
h	a	d	i	r	t	y	n	x	c	v	a
s	t	r	o	n	g	w	e	a	k	u	j
a	c	u	g	l	y	h	a	p	p	y	v
d	w	a	n	g	r	y	y	a	j	i	z
i	m	n	l	o	n	g	k	x	o	a	l
e	p	o	m	a	a	y	t	j	o	q	i

2 Match the opposites.

beautiful	cold
short	weak
strong	ugly
hot	long
clean	happy
angry	dirty

3 Read and answer the questions.

This word refers to the shape. A ball, a button and a plate are: r o u n d .

When you win a competition you are: f _ _ _ _ _ .

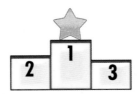

When you don't have enough sleep you are: t _ _ _ _ _ .

Windows and boxes are this shape. s _ _ _ _ _ _ .

When you want to eat something you are: h _ _ _ _ _ _ _ .

30

My Things

4 Match the words and pictures.

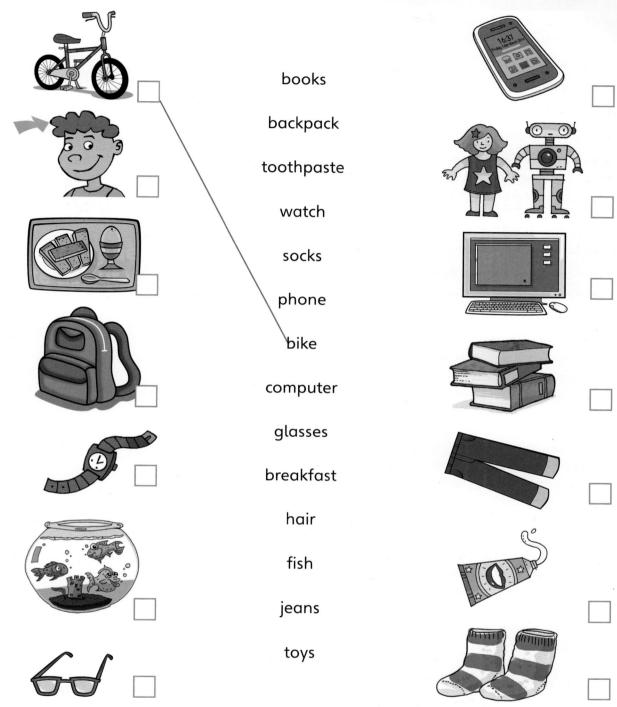

books

backpack

toothpaste

watch

socks

phone

bike

computer

glasses

breakfast

hair

fish

jeans

toys

5 Tick the things you have.

6 Tell your family about your things.

I like … .

My favourite
… is / are … .

It is / They
are. (colour)

31

The author would like to thank her friends and colleagues at the British Council, Naples for their support.

The author and publisher would like to thank the ELT professionals who reviewed the material at different stages of development: Lisa McNamara, Spain; Sarah Moore, Italy; Duygu Ozkankilic, Turkey; Jessica Smith, Italy.

Freelance Editorial Services by Trish Burrow.

Design and typeset by Wild Apple Design.

Cover design and header artwork by Chris Saunders (Astound).

Sound recordings by dsound Recording Studios, London.

The authors and publishers acknowledge the following sources of copyright material and are grateful for the permissions granted. While every effort has been made, it has not always been possible to identify the sources of all the material used, or to trace all copyright holders. If any omissions are brought to our notice, we will be happy to include the appropriate acknowledgements on reprinting and in the next update to the digital edition, as applicable.

The publishers are grateful to the following for permission to reproduce copyright photographs and material

Key: L = Left, C = Centre, R = Right, T = Top, B = Below, B/G = Background

Laetitia Aynié (Sylvie Poggio Artists Agency) pp. 14(B), 30(B) button, winner, window; David Banks pp. 8(T), 25; Joanna Boccardo 21(T); Bridget Dowty pp. 22(B) books; Chris Embleton-Hall (Advocate Art) pp. p15, 22(T) desk, write, draw, 22(B) dog, 23 (B); Andrew Elkerton (Sylvie Poggio Artists Agency) pp. 2, 3(B), 24(B), 28(T), 31 books; Clive Goodyer (Beehive Illustration) pp. 4(B), 23(T), 24(T), 30(T), 31 watch, computer, doll and robot, jeans, toothpaste; Andrew Hamilton @Elephant Shoes Ink Ltd pp. p17 (T), 20 ride a bike, 29, 31 breakfast, fish, glasses; Brett Hudson (Graham-Cameron Illustration) pp. 4(T), 18(B) sailing, swimming, 19(T) hockey, ice skating, piano, swimming, table tennis, 20 ride a horse; Kelly Kennedy (Sylvie Poggio Artists Agency) pp. 14(T); Nigel Kitching pp. 4(T), 5(B) splodges, 12, 13, 17(B), 31 hair; Andrew Painter: pp. 18(B) shopping, 27(T), 31 bike; Jamie Pogue @Bright Group pp. 16, 26, 27(B), 29; Nina de Polonia pp. 3(T), 19(T) playground, hospital, park, 20 sail; Andreas Ricci pp. 8(B), 19(T) comics, 22(T) board 30(B) tired girl, 31 mobile phone; Anthony Rule pp. 7, 11(B), 31 bag, socks; Pip Sampson pp. 18(T), 28(B); Melanie Sharp (Sylvie Poggio Artists Agency) pp. 5(B), 18(B) texting, 21(B), 22(B) story book; Sue Woollatt (Graham-Cameron Illustration) pp. 10, 11(T) (C), 22(T) playground, 25 (B).